750

Bluebirds Seven

paintings by R. Bruce Horsfall

text by Carra E. Horsfall

Preface

In 1917, R. Bruce Horsfall, a nationally recognized naturalist and bird artist with ties to the Oregon Audubon Society, painted a magnificent series of 33 water colors depicting Western Bluebirds. These dramatic and charming works of art, along with the story text by his wife, Carra E. Horsfall, and the original pen and ink drawings have lain forgotten for more than half a century. In the course of a recent cleaning at Portland's Audubon House, the drawings, text and paintings came to light.

The discovery occurred at a time when there was broad interest in efforts to restore Western Bluebirds to the numbers they once held in the Willamette Valley and the adjoining foothills. Forty years ago, bluebirds were common in the vicinity of Portland. Today they are rare even during the spring and summer, except in a few favored rural localities. The cause for the decline has been much speculated upon; it seems clear that one reason is the birds' inability to compete with House Sparrows, Starlings and Violet-green Swallows for cavity nesting sites. It is also possible that the ecological niche occupied by Western Bluebirds has been subtly encroached upon by other species, particularly in competition for wintertime food. It is also likely that the increased use of pesticides in orchards has contributed to the decline of the species. The Western Bluebird ranges west of the Rocky Mountains from southern British Columbia and central Montana into Mexico; nowhere does it seem to be as numerous as it once was.

Ken Batchelder

Kenneth C. Batchelder
Audubon Society of Portland

Mother and Father Bluebird lived in a box
on the window sill.
It was a comfortable, roomy birdhouse.

They worked hard carrying soft straws
and bits of string to make a cozy nest.
At last it was finished.

On Wednesday a beautiful blue egg was laid.

On Friday there was another.
By the middle of the next week five smooth
warm eggs were nestled under
the Mother Bluebird's downy breast.
For two weeks she kept them warm.

Then, "Pip, pip, peck, peck,"
a little beak tapped on the inside of an egg.
Crack went the shell.
After one breath of air, the baby Bluebird rested.
Then he began to squirm and wiggle and twist
until the shell was entirely broken.

How excited Mother Bluebird was!
How she hurried about
carrying away bits of broken shell
so that her house would be entirely clean.

Soon another shell pipped,
then another, and another
until five baby Bluebirds were lying in the nest.
Such little pink babies
without a single feather anywhere about them!

Now both Father and Mother Bluebird
were busy every minute,
hunting juicy worms, fat flies,
and dainty grubs for the five hungry babies.

How fast the babies ate those delicious morsels!
How fast those baby Bluebirds grew!
First came soft down and then blue feathers.

And how wonderful those feathers were!
There were fluffy ones to keep them warm.
They grew in rows down the middle of the back
and on each side of the breast.
They spread out and covered the little bodies
with soft down comforters.

The strong wing feathers grew more slowly.
They need to be light and flexible.
Each feather had a hollow quill edged with featherlets
held together so closely by tiny hooks
that neither air nor water could get through.

Every baby Bluebird wears the family coat of arms
during his first summer.
His family is the thrush family
and his coat of arms is a spotted vest.

Mother and Father Bluebird were so busy
finding food for their babies
that the little ones had no names for a week.
Then early one morning,
as Father Bluebird looked through the doorway he said,
"I think these children are old enough to be named."
"So do I," agreed Mother Bluebird
from her place on the edge of the nest,
"Let's call these two, Shortwing and Bobtail."
"And I shall name the rest —
Sleepy, Stuffy and Knownothing,"
answered Father Bluebird.

Knownothing always bobbed his head the wrong way when Father Bluebird had an especially wiggly earthworm for him.

Stuffy gobbled more fat grubs than any of the others.

Sleepy was annoyed
to be disturbed when she was napping.

Shortwing and Bobtail
were slow getting their long feathers.

But it was no time at all
before every one of them was anxious to try flying.
When they had talked it over beforehand,
each was eager to be the first one out of the nest.
But when the time came it was different.
"You go first." said Stuffy to Shortwing.
"No, you." said Shortwing to Bobtail.
But Bobtail thought Sleepy had better try it first.
"Oh, no, I need to take another nap."
She yawned and settled back into the nest.

"Aw who's afraid?" sang out Knownothing as he crowded past the others to the doorway and blundered out.

Down he went.
But he spread his wings just in time
to save himself from a terrible thump.
As it was, he landed rather heavily.

Mother Bluebird fluttered above him anxiously.
When she found that he was not hurt,
she coaxed him to a low bush nearby
and give him a fine big beetle.

Shortwing and Bobtail had done exercises
every day to help them grow.
They tried flying next.
Shortwing stretched her wings just as far as she could.
Then she flopped them and flopped them
and flopped them
until she reached a tree not far away.
Bobtail was soon beside her.

Stuffy and Sleepy were in the nest-box.
Such a commotion!
With three babies outside and two in the nest,
Mother and Father Bluebird were just about distracted.
Everyone was hungry at once!

This would never do.

Father said firmly, "No more worms for Stuffy
as long as he stays in the nest."

Stuffy cried and pouted. It did no good.

"You must come out," demanded Father Bluebird.

And he held a dainty white moth
just out of Stuffy's reach.

Stuffy was so hungry, and the moth looked so good,
that he forgot everything else and reached out to take it.

He lost his balance.

Plump, he went right to the ground.

He was so soft and fat it did not hurt him much.

Father Bluebird was there in an instant and rewarded him with the delicious moth. This pleased Stuffy so much that he gladly followed Father to the tree.

Sleepy begged for one more nap.
Mother Bluebird was quite out of patience.
She hopped into the nest, went behind Sleepy
and gave her a good hard push.
Out went the astonished baby.
But she spread her wings
and glided gently to the ground.
Then she refused to budge.
Father coaxed and Mother scolded
but there she stayed, determined to have another nap.
She did—but it was a very short one.

A gray form crept along beneath the bushes.
A great gray paw stretched out.
Sharp claws were extended.
Down they came—just as
someone said, "Scat!"
Everyone jumped.
The cat was gone in an instant.

Sleepy was very much awake now
but she had lost two of her tail feathers.
Sleepy hopped and flew until she reached the branch
where Bobtail and Shortwing were already perched.
Father and Mother Bluebird were more than glad to have
all their children safe together.

That night the whole family slept
on the arm of a telephone pole.
They had trouble getting settled
for each one wanted a place beside the pole.

The next day was a busy one, and the next, and the next.
There was much to learn about bathing;
about gathering food for themselves;
about watching for cats and dogs,
and about a very few children who had never learned
to love their bird friends and
who sometimes threw sticks and stones.

On a cool autumn day they had visitors.
Many Bluebirds called.
There was talk of a long journey.
Of course the five baby Bluebirds were all excited.
They had heard their parents speak of the fall flocking.
This must be it! Sure enough it was,
for soon they all started off together.
By easy flights they reached the Southland.
Here they spent a few pleasant months
away from the cold and snow and wintry weather.

But Spring came again to the northern garden
and so did the Bluebirds.
Straight to the box on the window sill.
Home again!
Before long there were five other Bluebird homes
in the neighborhood.
Shortwing, Bobtail, Sleepy, Stuffy and
Knownothing were raising families of their own.

About the Artist

R. Bruce Horsfall
  (1868-1948)

A professional artist, having studied in Europe, R. Bruce Horsfall painted habitat backgrounds for the American Museum of Natural History in New York City. Bird lovers of the Northwest became acquainted with his paintings for the Willard Ayres Eliot book *Birds of the Pacific Coast.*

While living in Portland, Oregon, he constructed a bluebird nesting box on a window sill of his home. A cardboard backing provided privacy for the birds until the young were hatched, thereafter it was withdrawn.

The birds seemed not to mind. Mr. Horsfall now viewed their activities and *Bluebirds Seven* came into being.

Acknowledgements

This book has been made possible through the generous donations and talents of many individuals. The paintings and original manuscript were given to the Audubon Society of Portland by members of the Horsfall family.

The Society's Director, Michael G. Uthoff, discovered the paintings and recognized their value. For editing the manuscript we thank Dr. Vera D. Petersen of Portland State University; for layout and graphic design, Martha Gannett; for encouragement with promotion and sales, Katharine McCanna of Far West Book Service.

Thanks also to Kenneth C. Batchelder, Chairman of the Book Committee, for his enthusiastic promotion of the project. Advice from Alice Butler for the financial arrangements was invaluable. Committee members assisting included John B. Crowell, Jr., James G. Olson, Harry B. Nehls, and Jeff Gilligan. Publication was accomplished with the approval of Audubon Society of Portland's officers and board of directors.